THE PATH OF THE VICTOR

Copyright © 2020 by Sam Rosenberg
All rights reserved.

ISBN 978-1-7344277-5-2 (print)
ISBN 978-1-7344277-6-9 (eBook)

Global Protective Services, Inc.
Pittsburgh, PA

www.GlobalProtective.Services

Design by Anna Hall

for Chrissy

INTRODUCTION

This book began as a simple statement of the philosophy behind the martial art I teach and which I have spent some twenty years developing. Somewhere along the way, however, it became a personal testament—a statement of the way I have come to view life and the code by which I try to live.

The ideas contained in these pages are in no way original. Rather, they're the distillation of the teaching of many victors who taught me—and the generations of victors who came before them, stretching all the way back to the 300 who stood at Thermopylae and refused to accept defeat.

For all the victors for whom the philosophy resonates, I salute you. May this book stand as a reminder that, although we are few, we are out there, bound together in a common mission.

May you follow the path of the victor to the end of your days.

—Sam Rosenberg

> "It is one thing to study war,
> and another to live the warrior's life."

—Telamon of Arcadia

MERCENARY, FIFTH CENTURY B.C.E.

There are two essential paths through life:

The path of the VICTIM and the path of the VICTOR.

The one we choose determines who we become. It also influences how we see the world and how the world perceives us.

Though they are unaware they are making this choice, most people choose the path of the VICTIM.

This is inevitably the path of least resistance.

It is seductive—easy at first, yet more treacherous with each succeeding step. Once internalized, it becomes a habit almost impossible to break.

The path of the VICTOR, by contrast, is hard to walk at first. It demands discipline, tenacity, and courage.

Yet the greatest rewards to be found in life are only available to those who are willing to choose this path.

The victim's journey is a largely external one, like that of a feather tossed on the seas of circumstance.

Lacking mastery of the self, the victim is unable to respond to events and shape them to his aims.

Instead, the victim reacts to circumstance, imposing a fictive veneer upon reality.

The path of the victor is an inward journey,
a path of self-mastery.

The victor does not seek to master others,
but rather, to master himself.

The victim sees life as governed by an inherent mechanism of fairness. He believes that everyone is entitled to their fair share of life's benefits.

Thus, the victim's thinking becomes controlled
by an illusion of entitlement.

The victor, by contrast, makes no presumptions about the world's fairness or lack thereof.

He creates his success
through the effort of his own hands.

He asks for nothing from the world
beyond the opportunities it presents.

THE VICTIM
sees difficulties
as obstacles to his entitled rewards.

◆

THE VICTOR
sees difficulties
as the opportunities
through which he creates success.

The victim confuses stability and routine
with success, peace, and tranquility.

So that he need not worry
about adapting to new challenges,
he leads a rote, predictable life.

The victim believes
that he may achieve certainty
through the accumulation of money,
and that his choice of neighborhood and home
are all he needs to remain safe
and to protect those he loves.

At the extreme,
the victim embraces the expectation
that someone will always be there to take care of him.

This certainty, this safety, and this expectation
are illusions.

The victor does not confuse success
with the accumulation of material things,
nor with the illusion of permanence.

He recognizes that the only quality he can rely on
is his ability to respond and adapt
to different circumstances.

He recognizes that success is a journey,
not a fixed condition.

Success to the victor
is the progressive realization of a worthy ideal.

That ideal, moreover, cannot be measured by any standards except those of the victor himself.

The victor understands that such peace is illusory.

Real peace is an inner state, not an external condition, a state that can only be reached by walking the path of the victor.

This peace, moreover, can and does exist
even in the midst of conflict.

The victor must learn to be an observer, as well as a participant.

The ability to stand apart
from the majority—
from the fear, conflict,
    and external conditions
that define most of the world—
is the first skill a victor must master,
the first step on the path to
    INNER PEACE.

The victim believes that the absence of difficulty and conflict is an end unto itself, and something to which his participation in a modern, democratic society somehow entitles him.

When this end is thwarted, therefore, the victim wallows in self-pity.

He convinces himself that life is "unfair."

Confronted with conflict, the victim turns fear into a constant psychological condition.

Conflict to the victim is something to be feared, loathed, despised, and avoided at all costs.

Even in the protection of life from aggression,
the victim often blames his protector
equally as his aggressor.

He creates a delusional world of moral equivalence,
one in which policemen
are indistinguishable from criminals;
one in which soldiers
are indistinguishable from terrorists.

Both are, to him, equally violent,
and thus equally culpable.

M oreover, he makes this fear so much a part of his consciousness that he is unable in time to distinguish between natural, instinctual fear and his "normal" state of timidity and denial.

By reacting to fear for so long that it becomes internalized, the victim blinds himself to any reality that does not conform to his notions of fairness and entitlement.

He lives his life inside a bubble of denial.

The victor, by contrast, refuses to deny reality,
no matter how unpleasant the manner in which it presents itself.

He welcomes his fear, because he understands precisely what it represents: valuable information by which he may organize his response to an uncomfortable reality.

In this way, fear becomes the victor's "sixth sense." It gives him valuable intelligence
on which to base his actions.

The victor accepts fear,
but he does not internalize it.

He looks on it as his squire, his spotter,
his faithful companion and guide.

By using his fear to deny reality, the victim also denies himself the precious knowledge
that could save his life.

Indeed, he puts himself further at the mercy
of the malevolent forces that drive him into panic.

But who can truly know peace?

The victim who fears conflict
without the means to overcome it?

Or the victor trained to meet
aggression head on, should the
need arise?

Throughout history, conflict,
violence, and aggression have been
part of the human condition.

The victor does not seek to overturn
this fact or imagine human nature
will ever change.

Rather, he seeks to hold the forces of
aggression in check through the
judicious application of force.

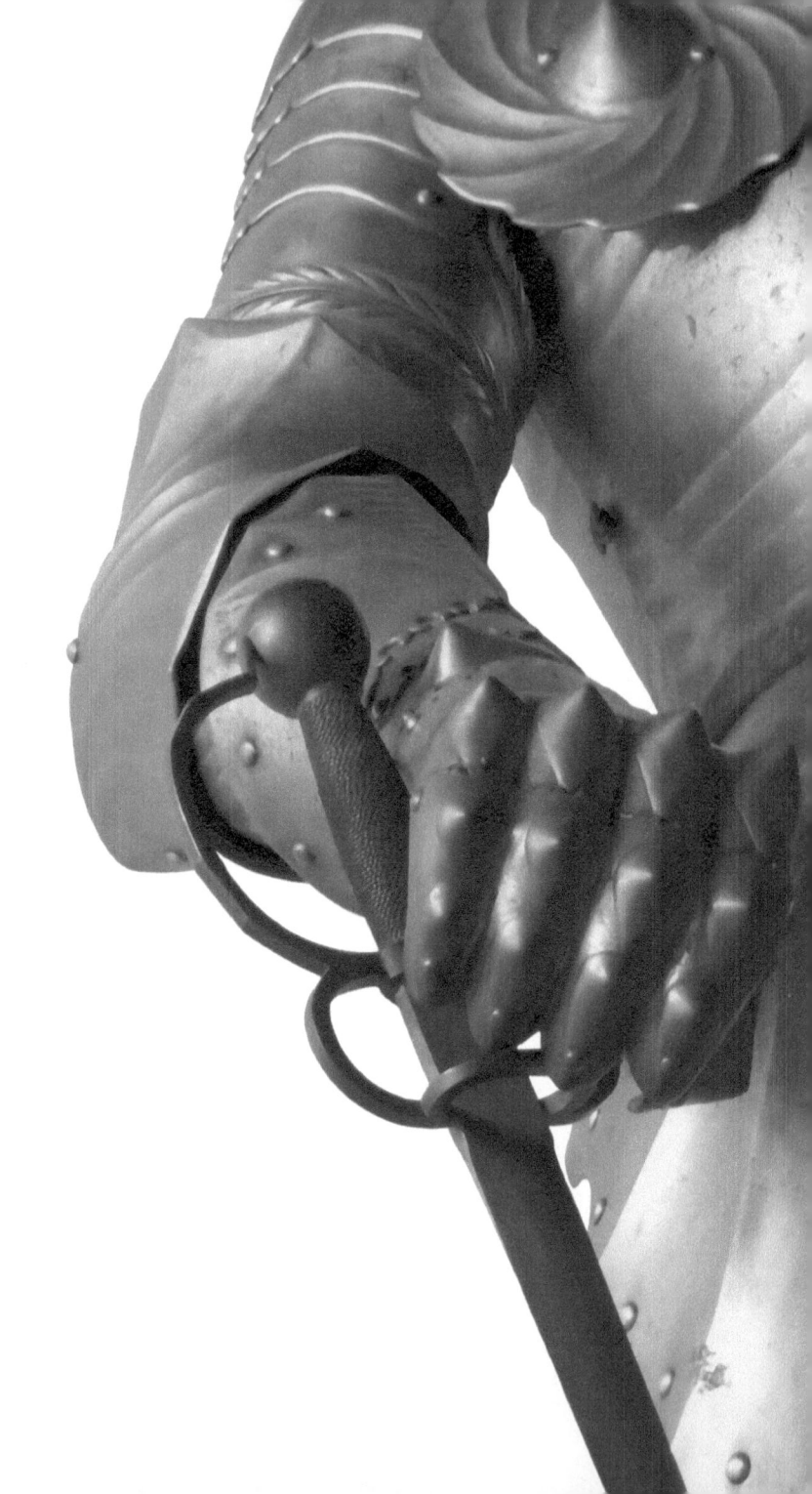

Taken by itself,
force is neither good nor evil.

What gives force its moral coloration
is its application—whether to
protect and preserve
or to dominate and destroy.

A victor never seeks to exert power
over others.
His ability to use force exists strictly to
allow him
to stay on his path
and to protect those weaker than
himself.

Though the victim
   may look upon the victor
with scorn and disdain,
his attitude is not reciprocated.

The victor views those under his
   protection with understanding and
   compassion,
just as a shepherd would his flock.

Death represents the victim's greatest single fear.

He seeks refuge from the thought of death in many forms: denial, diversion, superstition.

The victor who understands the
essential impermanence of
the physical world
has no fear of death.

To him, death is only another form of
change, another step along the path.

Death is what links every living thing,
and it is normal to feel the loss
of those we love acutely.

Yet death, in itself, has no meaning.

Meaning is something we discover and
attain only through living, through
following the steps
of life's journey.

Thus, in the victor's eyes,
it matters only how he has chosen to live,
not how death has overtaken him.

What is there then to fear?
Death, failure, humiliation?

The victor fears none of these.

Humiliation depends purely
on the opinions of others.

To the victor,
only the crucible of his own opinion matters.

Failure?

To the victor,
there is no such thing as success or failure,
only action and result.

Even death is not to be feared. We all die.
It is how we live that matters.

In the end, it comes down to this:
Did we live our lives freely,
according to the values of the victor,
or as a prisoner of victimhood?

THE SEVEN VIRTUES OF THE
VICTOR

The victor understands
 that impermanence and conflict
are not evidence that life lacks meaning.

The meaning is to be found in the
 path itself,
not in its presumed destination.

Though the path of each victor
leads to unique challenges and
 encounters;
and though the path of each victor
is guided by its own philosophies;
the path of every victor
follows the same essential guideposts.

These guideposts,
The Seven Virtues of the Victor,

shine the lamp of right thought
to illuminate the way of right action.

Without them,
the victor stumbles and loses the path.

With each step,
the Seven Virtues
progressively reveal the way.

Thus, the journey becomes its own reward.

THE FIRST VIRTUE
DISCIPLINE

DISCIPLINE
is the foremost quality of the victor.

This virtue is the first and most
obvious line of separation between
the victor
and the victim.

It is said that if you don't know where you are going, any road will take you there.

This saying perfectly describes the way of the victim.

In this fashion, the victim rejects
the path of discipline
that marks the beginning of the victor's way.

He seeks pleasure, while avoiding difficulty and pain.

He convinces himself that the conflict the victor embraces is an aberration to be ignored
or avoided whenever possible.

Thus, he refuses to discipline himself
to deal with inevitable conflict
and follows the path of avoidance, fear, and denial.

To the victor,
 discipline means that every
 action is a conscious choice, not a
 reaction to the behavior of others.

Mindful action originates in careful
 preparation and training, handed
 down from one victor to another.

These traditions connect generations
 of victors
in a single family.

The victor understands that discipline,
like the inertia of a bicycle,
is what keeps him balanced, directed,
 and moving forward on the path.

When discipline lapses,
he loses both his balance and his way.

It becomes all too easy to drift
toward the path of the victim,
the way of aimlessness.

The victor understands
that true discipline cannot be
imposed from outside.

Only self-discipline can keep the
victor on the path.

Discipline, rightly understood,
is not shaped by external ideology
but by the inner truth the victor gains
through training and experience.

THE SECOND VIRTUE
INDEPENDENCE

INDEPENDENCE
is the second virtue of the victor.

The true victor maintains his
independence
from the ideologies of others.

He treasures freedom of thought and
action—
and works to preserve and nurture
this freedom wherever it is found.

The victim looks to the opinion of others
to validate his own actions
and his own sense of self-worth.

In doing so, he enslaves himself to
the common view and cripples
his own capacity
for creative thought and action.

A victor understands that only he is responsible
for his own thoughts and acts.

He accepts the result of his actions
and does not blame them on others.

In pursuit of independence,
the victor must carve his own way.
In so doing, he will sometimes stumble.

The victor understands
that falling is far superior to veering,
that setbacks are acceptable,
but that a loss of discipline is not.

Ever the victor keeps his focus
on the act of advancing,
and on the reward that is the journey.

THE THIRD VIRTUE
RESPECT

No one, even the most enlightened master,
is immune from mistakes.

The victor understands this. He is accepting of both his own faults and the faults of others.

In this acceptance, he develops compassion.

He pursues the third virtue:
RESPECT.

The victim,
   clinging to his notions of
   entitlement,
lacks respect for others, for his
   environment,
and even for himself.

He becomes the prisoner
of what he believes others owe him,
and he forgets the debt he owes to
   others.

He thus walls himself off from his
   environment,
from the web of interconnectedness.

Thus are planted the seeds of his
   demise.

Respect, to the victor,
is a function of this compassion,
not a blind adherence to the social
 conventions
of a given time and place.

He understands that all things are
 interconnected,
and those relationships stretch
 beyond
the ability of human understanding.

As such, he strives to maintain his
 beginner's mind, and to learn
 from all he encounters.

Ultimately,
the victor knows that most things
lie beyond his control or influence.

In this awareness, he learns to respect
all he encounters
in nature and in life.

THE FOURTH VIRTUE
STEADFASTNESS

The promise of convenience,
the allure of comfort,
the persuasive sense of entitlement—
these do not sway the victor.

Neither does the distraction of fear,
nor the negative opinions of others,
nor the wavering influence of doubt.

Along the way,
the journey will offer many
opportunities
to forget the path and leave it behind.

It is a law of nature akin to gravity.
If you do not fight its pull,
then it will pull you down.

The victor ever keeps his feet on the
path,
for he adheres to the virtue of
STEADFASTNESS.

The victim,
   seduced by the path of ease and entitlement,
will endeavor to pull the victor off the path.

He strives to refashion the victor in his own image.

The victor learns to cultivate the habit of Steadfastness
to remain on the path
regardless of the prevailing climate of opinion.

The victor accepts hardship and suffering
as not only a necessary condition of the path, but a universal condition.

To endure suffering, the victor has learned to find meaning within.

In this acceptance, steadfastly walking the path
builds the endurance that enables
the continuation of the journey.

The journey becomes the meaning,
and the meaning becomes the journey.

THE FIFTH VIRTUE
DECISIVENESS

We are not born fearful,
but most become conditioned to be afraid—
of the judgment of others,
and of making wrong decisions.

This fear causes them to eschew responsibility,
and to allow others to take the lead.

Paradoxically, they are also afraid
of being right,
or of taking charge,
for with these conditions
comes the burden of responsibility.

While others follow this indecision
into a state of paralysis,
the victor demonstrates his capacity to take action—
even when the right action is to take no action—
for his is the Fifth Virtue
of DECISIVENESS.

The victim,
 unsure of himself
and fearful of taking responsibility for
 his actions
wallows in indecision and uncertainty.

The victor
 cultivates decisiveness
and strives to make it a habit.

Though he understands
that all judgment is imperfect,
he does not shy from bold decisions.

This quality is what separates him
 most obviously from the victim.

It takes great discipline
and a long period of experience
and training
to foster a consistent confidence
to quickly decide and then act.

For the victor, the key is knowing
and accepting
that sometimes decisions and actions
will be wrong.

This does not mean that the victor
acts impulsively.

Foolish action is never tolerated.

But he learns to rely on the
information available,
to trust his intuition,
and to make decisions where others
might devolve into a state of
inaction.

THE SIXTH VIRTUE
INTEGRITY

INTEGRITY
is the root of all pursuits.

Without a proper foundation,
even the most inspiring structures will fall.

Any endeavor,
if it is to be successful, celebrated,
and able to stand on its own,
will demonstrate integrity.

Thus, the victor maintains
the Sixth Virtue,
Integrity in all things.

The victim
   who allows others to shape his
   image of himself
has no ability to understand his true self
nor to act in accordance with it.

His estimation of himself is,
   in every sense,
delusional.

The victor understands
the essential unity of thought and action.

He is honest with himself
and behaves in accordance with this reality.

For the victor, the Sixth Virtue of Integrity
is about more than simple honesty.
It is about doing what is right at all times.

Integrity is not blind allegiance to authority.
If an order is unlawful or unjust,
Integrity guides the victor to disobey.

Neither is Integrity
a stubborn adherence to independence.

Integrity is what centers the victor on the right path;
it is the continuous reinforcement
of his own strong foundation.

THE SEVENTH VIRTUE
DETATCHMENT

Whether presented with conflict,
with setback, with tragedy,
or with illness,
one cannot choose the battles one
must fight.

Some of these battles,
we will win.
Some of these battles,
we will lose.

What matters is that we do not allow
these battles
to deter us from the path.

It is for this reason that
DETACHMENT FROM OUTCOME
is the highest virtue of the victor.

In any battle,
the trap is in losing focus on the moment.

The victim gets caught up in the concern
over victory or defeat.

The moment the weight of that assessment
falls upon him,
he is already fighting himself,
and thus,
he is already defeated.

The victor recognizes
that victory and defeat are illusions—
states of mind predicated on perspective.

Thus, Detachment
allows him to perform at his best,
because his focus remains exclusively
on performing and not on concern over the outcome.

By removing the fear of defeat,
by eliminating the desire
for the gratification that comes with victory,
and by ignoring concern over others' opinions,
the victor may engage with his battles
to the best of his ability.

Whether standing up for a principle,
living his highest self,
or facing the storm of other people's ridicule,
the victor knows the freedom of pursuing his dreams.

Ultimately, none of us is entitled
to the fruits of our labor—
only to our labor.

No matter how we may try,
we cannot control every outcome;
we can only influence them.

The best way to fight, therefore,
is to achieve Detachment from
    Outcome.

It is this Detachment
that allows us the chance
to always do the right thing,
to grow with every battle,
and to stay the path.

Through the cultivation of

DISCIPLINE,
INDEPENDENCE,
RESPECT,
STEADFASTNESS,
DECISIVENESS,
INTEGRITY,
and DETACHMENT,

the victor arrives at the state known as *equanimity*.

He is unshaken by circumstance.

He experiences fear yet remains unafraid.

He is surrounded by turmoil yet remains at peace.

Even in defeat, he remains undefeated.

In following the path of the victor, he finds INNER PEACE.

 A former Marine officer and professional bodyguard, Sam Rosenberg today works as a personal security trainer and consultant. His lifelong study of human violence and aggression led him to develop a practical approach to managing physical conflict in the real world.

Based in Pittsburgh, PA, Sam teaches personal defensive tactics to a diverse clientele, ranging from celebrities, professional athletes, and business executives to schoolchildren and victims of violent crime.

www.ingramcontent.com/pod-product-compliance
Lightning Source LLC
Chambersburg PA
CBHW021121080526
44587CB00010B/592